G000016038

DIARY

2006

VICTORIA
AND ALBERT
MUSEUM

FRANCES LINCOLN

Frances Lincoln Limited
4 Torriano Mews
Torriano Avenue
London NW5 2RZ
www.franceslincoln.com

British Library cataloguing-in-publication data
A catalogue record for this book is available from
the British Library

ISBN 0-7112-2513-3

Printed in China

First Frances Lincoln edition 2005

Cover: The 'Helena' furnishing fabric, designed by C.F.A.
Voysey (1857–1941) and manufactured by Alexander
Morton & Co. Silk and wool double cloth. English,
1895–1900.

Title page: Painted and gilded mahogany case clock,
designed and painted by C.F.A. Voysey (1857–1941) with
brass and steel movement made by Camerer, Cuss & Co.
and case made by Frederick Coote. English, 1895–1896.

Overleaf: Stained oak 'Argyle' chair, designed by Charles
Rennie Mackintosh (1868–1928). Scottish, 1897–1900.

VISITORS' INFORMATION
The Victoria and Albert Museum
Cromwell Road
South Kensington, London SW7 2RL
Telephone: 020 7942 2000

Museum hours of opening: daily 10 am to 5.45 pm
Closed: Christmas Eve, Christmas Day and Boxing Day
Late View opening until 10 pm: every Wednesday and
the last Friday in every month

For information on the V&A Museum, please visit the
website on www.vam.ac.uk. For information on V&A
inspired products, please visit the V&A Museum shop
website on www.vandashop.co.uk.

For information on joining the Friends of the V&A, please
contact the Friends Office on 020 7942 2271

CALENDAR 2006

JANUARY	FEBRUARY	MARCH	APRIL	MAY	JUNE
M T W T F S S	M T W T F S S	M T W T F S S	M T W T F S S	M T W T F S S	M T W T F S S
1	1 2 3 4 5	1 2 3 4 5	1 2	1 2 3 4 5 6 7	1 2 3 4
2 3 4 5 6 7 8	6 7 8 9 10 11 12	6 7 8 9 10 11 12	3 4 5 6 7 8 9	8 9 10 11 12 13 14	5 6 7 8 9 10 11
9 10 11 12 13 14 15	13 14 15 16 17 18 19	13 14 15 16 17 18 19	10 11 12 13 14 15 16	15 16 17 18 19 20 21	12 13 14 15 16 17 18
16 17 18 19 20 21 22	20 21 22 23 24 25 26	20 21 22 23 24 25 26	17 18 19 20 21 22 23	22 23 24 25 26 27 28	19 20 21 22 23 24 25
23 24 25 26 27 28 29	27 28	27 28 29 30 31	24 25 26 27 28 29 30	29 30 31	26 27 28 29 30
30 31					

JULY	AUGUST	SEPTEMBER	OCTOBER	NOVEMBER	DECEMBER
M T W T F S S	M T W T F S S	M T W T F S S	M T W T F S S	M T W T F S S	M T W T F S S
1 2	1 2 3 4 5 6	1 2 3	1	1 2 3 4 5	1 2 3
3 4 5 6 7 8 9	7 8 9 10 11 12 13	4 5 6 7 8 9 10	2 3 4 5 6 7 8	6 7 8 9 10 11 12	4 5 6 7 8 9 10
10 11 12 13 14 15 16	14 15 16 17 18 19 20	11 12 13 14 15 16 17	9 10 11 12 13 14 15	13 14 15 16 17 18 19	11 12 13 14 15 16 17
17 18 19 20 21 22 23	21 22 23 24 25 26 27	18 19 20 21 22 23 24	16 17 18 19 20 21 22	20 21 22 23 24 25 26	18 19 20 21 22 23 24
24 25 26 27 28 29 30	28 29 30 31	25 26 27 28 29 30	23 24 25 26 27 28 29	27 28 29 30	25 26 27 28 29 30 31
31			30 31		

CALENDAR 2007

JANUARY	FEBRUARY	MARCH	APRIL	MAY	JUNE
M T W T F S S	M T W T F S S	M T W T F S S	M T W T F S S	M T W T F S S	M T W T F S S
1 2 3 4 5 6 7	1 2 3 4	1 2 3 4	1 2 3 4 5 6	1 2 3 4 5 6	1 2 3
8 9 10 11 12 13 14	5 6 7 8 9 10 11	5 6 7 8 9 10 11	2 3 4 5 6 7 8	7 8 9 10 11 12 13	4 5 6 7 8 9 10
15 16 17 18 19 20 21	12 13 14 15 16 17 18	12 13 14 15 16 17 18	9 10 11 12 13 14 15	14 15 16 17 18 19 20	11 12 13 14 15 16 17
22 23 24 25 26 27 28	19 20 21 22 23 24 25	19 20 21 22 23 24 25	16 17 18 19 20 21 22	21 22 23 24 25 26 27	18 19 20 21 22 23 24
29 30 31	26 27 28	26 27 28 29 30 31	23 24 25 26 27 28 29	28 29 30 31	25 26 27 28 29 30
			30		

JULY	AUGUST	SEPTEMBER	OCTOBER	NOVEMBER	DECEMBER
M T W T F S S	M T W T F S S	M T W T F S S	M T W T F S S	M T W T F S S	M T W T F S S
1	1 2 3 4 5	1 2	1 2 3 4 5 6 7	1 2 3 4	1 2
2 3 4 5 6 7 8	6 7 8 9 10 11 12	3 4 5 6 7 8 9	8 9 10 11 12 13 14	5 6 7 8 9 10 11	3 4 5 6 7 8 9
9 10 11 12 13 14 15	13 14 15 16 17 18 19	10 11 12 13 14 15 16	15 16 17 18 19 20 21	12 13 14 15 16 17 18	10 11 12 13 14 15 16
16 17 18 19 20 21 22	20 21 22 23 24 25 26	17 18 19 20 21 22 23	22 23 24 25 26 27 28	19 20 21 22 23 24 25	17 18 19 20 21 22 23
23 24 25 26 27 28 29	27 28 29 30 31	24 25 26 27 28 29 30	29 30 31	26 27 28 29 30	24 25 26 27 28 29 30
30 31					31

INTRODUCTION

The Victoria and Albert Museum has one of the most important and wide-ranging Arts and Crafts collections in the world. One of the great figures who inspired the Arts and Crafts Movement was the designer, writer and activist William Morris, who was closely involved with the Museum. In 1865 his firm decorated the Green Dining Room, now known as the Morris Room, which is still today one of the splendours of the V&A building. The V&A has a comprehensive collection of his work in every medium, of which highlights can be seen in the British Galleries.

Alongside them, and beautifully illustrated here, is a selection of furniture, textiles, ceramics, metalwork and jewellery, designs and book illustrations by some of the greatest architects and designers of the Arts and Crafts Movement in Britain. Superb examples of objects from the international developments in the movement – from America, Germany, Austria, Hungary, Russia, Scandinavia and Japan – are also illustrated here and more can be found in the collections.

The Arts and Crafts Movement was one of the most far-reaching and influential design movements of modern times. It began in Britain, where it flourished between c.1880 and 1914, and quickly spread across America and Europe between c.1890 and 1916, emerging finally as the Mingei (Folk Crafts) movement in Japan between 1926 and 1945. It was a movement born of ideals, and it grew out of a concern for the effects of industrialisation on design, the loss of traditional skills and crafts, and the subsequent effect on the lives of ordinary working people. In response, the Arts and Crafts Movement established a new set of principles for living and working. It advocated the reform of art at every level and across a broad social spectrum, and it turned the home into a work of art. In every aspect the Arts and Crafts Movement changed the way we think about design for the home and how we value the way things are made, and its principles continue to have an impact on the world we live in today.

Karen Livingstone Curator

DECEMBER/JANUARY

6 MONDAY

Boxing Day (St Stephen's Day)
Holiday, UK, Republic of Ireland, Canada, USA,
Australia and New Zealand (Christmas Day observed)

27 TUESDAY

Holiday, UK, Republic of Ireland, Canada,
Australia and New Zealand (Boxing Day observed)

28 WEDNESDAY

29 THURSDAY

30 FRIDAY

31 SATURDAY

New Moon
New Year's Eve

1 SUNDAY

New Year's Day

Green glass decanter with silver mounts and a chrysophase
set in the finial, designed by C.R. Ashbee (1863–1942) and
manufactured by James Powell & Sons, London,
English, 1904–1905.

JANUARY

2 MONDAY

6 FRIDAY

Holiday, UK, Republic of Ireland, Canada,
USA, Australia and New Zealand

First Quarter
Epiphany

3 TUESDAY

7 SATURDAY

Holiday, Scotland and New Zealand

4 WEDNESDAY

8 SUNDAY

5 THURSDAY

Darmstadt, Die Ausstellung des Künstler-kolonie, poster designed
by Joseph Maria Olbrich (1867—1908) and printed by
H. Hohmann, Darmstadt. Colour lithograph. German, 1901.

UNTER · DEM · ALLERHÖCHSTEN · PROTECTORATE
SR · KÖNIGL · HOHEIT · DES · GROSHERZOGS · VON · HESSEN
EIN · DOKUMENT · DEUTSCHER · KUNST —

DARMSTADT

MAI — OCTOBER 1901
DIE · AUSSTELLUNG · DER

JANUARY

9 MONDAY

13 FRIDAY

10 TUESDAY

14 SATURDAY

Full Moon

11 WEDNESDAY

15 SUNDAY

12 THURSDAY

Silver butter knife, sugar sprinkler and dessert knife, designed
by C.R. Ashbee (1863–1942) and manufactured by the
Guild of Handicraft. English, 1900–1902.

16 MONDAY

20 FRIDAY

Holiday, USA (Martin Luther King's birthday)

17 TUESDAY

21 SATURDAY

18 WEDNESDAY

22 SUNDAY

Last Quarter

19 THURSDAY

The 'Peacock' sconce, designed and manufactured by
Alexander Fisher (1864–1936). Steel, bronze, brass and silver
with enamelled decoration. English, 1899.

23 MONDAY

27 FRIDAY

24 TUESDAY

28 SATURDAY

25 WEDNESDAY

29 SUNDAY

New Moon
Chinese New Year

26 THURSDAY

Holiday, Australia (Australia Day)

The 'Glastonbury' oak armchair, designed by A.W.N. Pugin
(1812–1852) and possibly made by George Myers
(1803–1875). English, 1839–1841.

JANUARY/FEBRUARY

30 MONDAY

3 FRIDAY

31 TUESDAY

4 SATURDAY

Islamic New Year (subject to sighting of the moon)

1 WEDNESDAY

5 SUNDAY

First Quarter

2 THURSDAY

Wall hanging, designed by A.H. Mackmurdo (1851–1942)
for the Century Guild and produced by A.H. Lee & Son.
Woven wool and cotton. English, about 1887–1888

6 MONDAY

10 FRIDAY

Holiday, New Zealand (Waitangi Day)

7 TUESDAY

11 SATURDAY

8 WEDNESDAY

12 SUNDAY

Lincoln's birthday

9 THURSDAY

The 'Well Spring' vase, designed in 1847 by Richard Redgrave
(1804–1888) and made by Minton & Co. for Felix Summerly's
Art Manufactures. Porcelain, painted in enamels. English, 1865.

FEBRUARY

13 MONDAY

Full Moon
Holiday (observed), USA

14 TUESDAY

St Valentine's Day

15 WEDNESDAY

16 THURSDAY

17 FRIDAY

18 SATURDAY

19 SUNDAY

Comb, designed by Joseph Hodel (1873–1930). Ivory
mounted in silver and set with mother-of-pearl, sapphire,
green-stained chalcedony and a fire opal matrix. English, 190

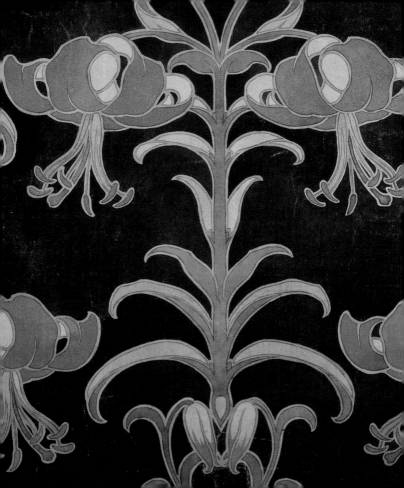

FEBRUARY

0 MONDAY

24 FRIDAY

Holiday, USA (Presidents' Day)

21 TUESDAY

25 SATURDAY

Last Quarter

22 WEDNESDAY

26 SUNDAY

23 THURSDAY

The 'Tiger Lily' design for a printed textile by Lindsay P. Butterfield (1869–1948). Pencil and watercolour on paper. English, 1896.

27 MONDAY

3 FRIDAY

28 TUESDAY

4 SATURDAY

New Moon
Shrove Tuesday

1 WEDNESDAY

5 SUNDAY

Ash Wednesday
St David's Day

2 THURSDAY

Clutha (cloudy) glass vase, designed by Christopher Dresser
(1834–1904) and manufactured by James Couper & Sons,
Glasgow. Scottish, 1885.

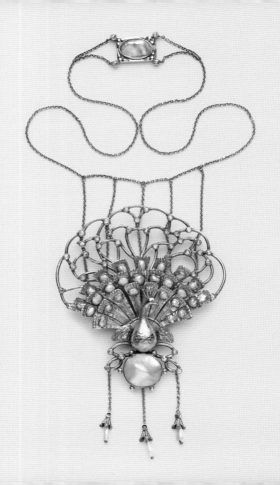

MARCH

6 MONDAY

10 FRIDAY

First Quarter

7 TUESDAY

11 SATURDAY

8 WEDNESDAY

12 SUNDAY

9 THURSDAY

Necklace, designed by C.R. Ashbee (1863–1942) for the
Guild of Handicraft. Silver and gold set with blister pearls,
diamond sparks and a demantoid garnet for the eye with
three pendant pearls. English, about 1901–1902.

13 MONDAY

17 FRIDAY

St Patrick's Day
Holiday, Northern Ireland and Republic of Ireland

Commonwealth Day

14 TUESDAY

18 SATURDAY

Full Moon

15 WEDNESDAY

19 SUNDAY

16 THURSDAY

Architectural drawing for the Red House by Philip Webb
(1831–1915). Pencil, pen ink and watercolour on paper
English, 1859

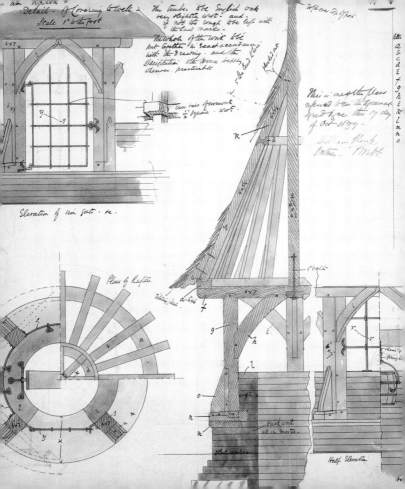

Detail · of Covering to Well

Scale 1" to the foot

Elevation of iron Gate · &c.

Plan of Rafters.

Half Elevation

THE STUDIO

AN ILLVSTRATED MAGAZINE
OF FINE AND APPLIED ART

MARCH

20 MONDAY

24 FRIDAY

Vernal Equinox

21 TUESDAY

25 SATURDAY

22 WEDNESDAY

26 SUNDAY

Mothering Sunday, UK
British Summertime begins

Last Quarter

23 THURSDAY

Advertisement for 'The Studio', designed by Aubrey Beardsley
(1872–1898). Line block and letterpress. English, 1893.

MARCH/APRIL

27 MONDAY

28 TUESDAY

1 SATURDAY

29 WEDNESDAY

2 SUNDAY

New Moon

30 THURSDAY

Cushion cover, designed by Jessie Newbery (1864–1948)
Linen ground with linen appliqué, embroidered with silk
Scottish, 1900

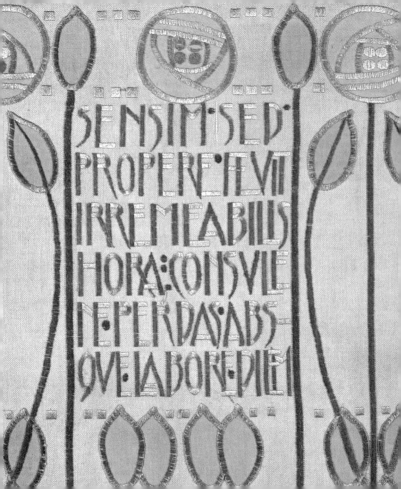

SENSIM SED
PROPERE FVIT
IRREMEABILIS
HORA: CONSVLE
TE PERDAS ABS
QVE LABORE DIEM

3 MONDAY

7 FRIDAY

4 TUESDAY

8 SATURDAY

5 WEDNESDAY

9 SUNDAY

First Quarter

Palm Sunday

6 THURSDAY

Armchair, designed by Josef Hoffman (1870–1956) and made
by the Wiener Werkstätte, Vienna. Steam-bent beechwood
frame with plywood seat and back. Austrian, 1905.

10 MONDAY

14 FRIDA

Good Frid
Holiday, UK, Republic of Irelan
Canada, USA, Australia and New Zealar

11 TUESDAY

15 SATURDA

12 WEDNESDAY

16 SUNDA

Easter Sunda

13 THURSDAY

Full Moon
Maundy Thursday
Passover (Pesach), First Day

The 'Daisy' tile, designed by William Morris (1834–189
and produced by Morris, Marshall, Faulkner & Co. Han
painted on tin-glazed earthenware. English, 1862–188

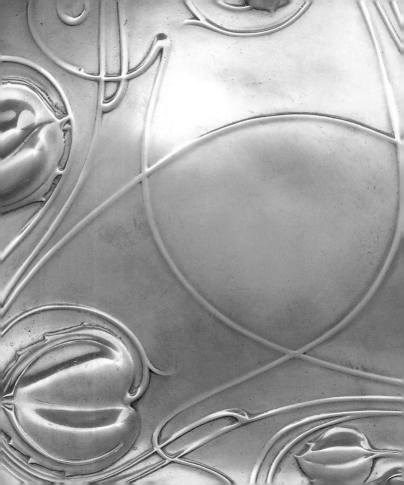

APRIL

7 MONDAY

21 FRIDAY

Easter Monday
Holiday, UK (exc. Scotland), Republic of Ireland,
Canada, Australia and New Zealand

Last Quarter
Birthday of Queen Elizabeth II

8 TUESDAY

22 SATURDAY

9 WEDNESDAY

23 SUNDAY

Passover (Pesach), Seventh Day

St George's Day

10 THURSDAY

Passover (Pesach), Eighth Day

Liberty pewter dish, designed by Archibald Knox (1864–1933)
and produced by W.H. Haseler, Birmingham. English, 1903.

24 MONDAY

28 FRIDA

25 TUESDAY

29 SATURDA

Holiday, Australia and New Zealand (Anzac Day)

26 WEDNESDAY

30 SUNDA

27 THURSDAY

New Moon

Earthenware vase, designed by Harriet Elizabeth Wilcox fi
Rockwood Pottery, Cincinnati. American, 190

MAY

1 MONDAY

5 FRIDAY

Early May Bank Holiday, UK and Republic of Ireland

First Quarter

2 TUESDAY

6 SATURDAY

3 WEDNESDAY

7 SUNDAY

4 THURSDAY

Cotton kimono with stencil-resist decoration (bingata).
Japanese (Okinawa), nineteenth century.

MAY

8 MONDAY

12 FRIDA

9 TUESDAY

13 SATURDA

Full Moc

10 WEDNESDAY

14 SUNDA

Mother's Day, Canada, USA, Australia and New Zealan

11 THURSDAY

Design for a wallpaper by C.F.A. Voysey (1857–1941)
Pencil, pen and black ink and watercolour. English, 190

MAY

15 MONDAY

19 FRIDAY

16 TUESDAY

20 SATURDAY

Last Quarter

17 WEDNESDAY

21 SUNDAY

18 THURSDAY

Stoneware vase with a high-temperature flambé glaze,
designed by William Howson Taylor (1876–1935) for the
Ruskin Pottery, Smethwick, near Birmingham. English, 1910.

MAY

22 MONDAY

26 FRID

23 TUESDAY

27 SATURD

New Mo

24 WEDNESDAY

28 SUND

25 THURSDAY

Ascension Day

Design for a woven silk by C.F.A. Voysey (1857–194
Pencil and watercolour on paper. English, 191

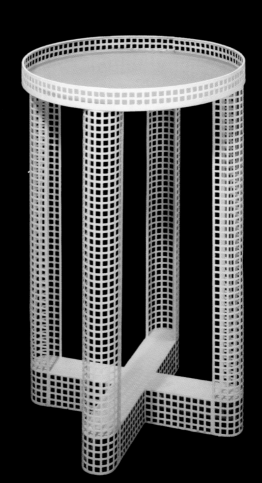

MAY/JUNE

9 MONDAY

2 FRIDAY

Spring Bank Holiday, UK
Holiday, USA (Memorial Day)

Jewish Feast of Weeks (Shavuot)

0 TUESDAY

3 SATURDAY

First Quarter

WEDNESDAY

4 SUNDAY

THURSDAY

Whit Sunday (Pentecost)

Painted iron flower table, designed by Josef Hoffman
(1870–1956) and made by the Wiener Werkstätte, Vienna.
Austrian, 1904.

JUNE

5 MONDAY

9 FRIDAY

Holiday, Republic of Ireland
Holiday, New Zealand (The Queen's birthday)

6 TUESDAY

10 SATURDAY

The Queen's official birthday (subject to confirmation)

7 WEDNESDAY

11 SUNDAY

Full Moon
Trinity Sunday

8 THURSDAY

Design for a wallpaper or printed textile by C.F.A. Voysey
(1857–1941). Pencil and watercolour on paper. English, 19

JUNE

2 MONDAY

16 FRIDAY

Holiday, Australia (The Queen's birthday)

3 TUESDAY

17 SATURDAY

4 WEDNESDAY

18 SUNDAY

Last Quarter
Father's Day, UK, Canada and USA

5 THURSDAY

Fruit basket, designed by Josef Hoffman (1870–1956)
and made by the Wiener Werkstätte, Vienna. Silver,
hammered and raised. Austrian, 1904.

Corpus Christi

JUNE

19 MONDAY

23 FRIDAY

20 TUESDAY

24 SATURDAY

21 WEDNESDAY

25 SUNDAY

Summer Solstice

22 THURSDAY

New Moon

Design for a wallpaper or printed textile by Lindsay P. Butterfield
(1869–1948). Pencil and watercolour on paper. English, 1903.

JUNE/JULY

6 MONDAY

30 FRIDAY

7 TUESDAY

1 SATURDAY

Holiday, Canada (Canada Day)

8 WEDNESDAY

2 SUNDAY

9 THURSDAY

Writing desk, designed by C.F.A. Voysey (1857–1941) for
William and Haydee Ward-Higgs, with metalwork by
W.B. Reynolds. Oak with brass panel and copper hinges.
English, 1896.

JULY

3 MONDAY

7 FRIDAY

First Quarter

4 TUESDAY

8 SATURDAY

Holiday, USA (Independence Day)

5 WEDNESDAY

9 SUNDAY

New Moon

6 THURSDAY

Design for a wallpaper by Lindsay P. Butterfield (1869–1948)
Pencil and watercolour on paper. English, 1901

MONDAY

14 FRIDAY

TUESDAY

15 SATURDAY

ll Moon

St Swithin's Day

2 WEDNESDAY

16 SUNDAY

Holiday, Northern Ireland (Battle of the Boyne)

3 THURSDAY

The 'Fools Parsley' design for a wallpaper by C.F.A. Voysey (1857–1941). Pencil and watercolour on paper. English, 1907.

17 MONDAY

21 FRIDAY

Last Quarter

18 TUESDAY

22 SATURDAY

19 WEDNESDAY

23 SUNDAY

20 THURSDAY

Liberty 'Cymric' cigarette box, designed by Archibald Knox (1864–1933) and produced by W.H. Haseler, Birmingham. Silver embossed and inlaid with opal matrix. English, about 1903–1904.

24 MONDAY

28 FRIDAY

25 TUESDAY

29 SATURDAY

New Moon

26 WEDNESDAY

30 SUNDAY

27 THURSDAY

The 'Saladin' furnishing fabric, designed by C.F.A. Voysey
(1857–1941). Printed cotton. English, 1897.

JULY / AUGUST

31 MONDAY

4 FRIDA

1 TUESDAY

5 SATURDA

2 WEDNESDAY

6 SUNDA

First Quarter

3 THURSDAY

Earthenware tile, hand-painted on a white slip, designed an
made by William De Morgan (1839–1917). English, 189

s
l
c
c
r
a
l
c
c
k

❧ It is of such a Press t
and in so doing to estimate
scheme of things, but als
character. The question

AUGUST

MONDAY

11 FRIDAY

Summer Bank Holiday, Scotland and Republic of Ireland

TUESDAY

12 SATURDAY

WEDNESDAY

13 SUNDAY

Full Moon

10 THURSDAY

Page from *The Private Press*, designed by C.R. Ashbee
(1863–1942). English, 1908.

AUGUST

14 MONDAY

18 FRIDAY

15 TUESDAY

19 SATURDAY

16 WEDNESDAY

20 SUNDAY

Last Quarter

17 THURSDAY

Stained and painted glass panel, designed by Selwyn Image
(1849–1930) and produced by Shrigley & Hunt, Lancashire.
English, 1884.

AUGUST

MONDAY

25 FRIDAY

TUESDAY

26 SATURDAY

WEDNESDAY

27 SUNDAY

New Moon

THURSDAY

Design for a wallpaper or printed textile by
Lindsay P. Butterfield (1869–1948).
Pencil and watercolour on paper. English, about 1900.

AUGUST / SEPTEMBER

28 MONDAY

1 FRID

Summer Bank Holiday, UK (exc. Scotland)

29 TUESDAY

2 SATURD

30 WEDNESDAY

3 SUND

Father's Day, Australia and New Zeala

31 THURSDAY

First Quarter

Earthenware vase with gilt and lustre decoration, designed
William De Morgan (1839–1917). English, about 189

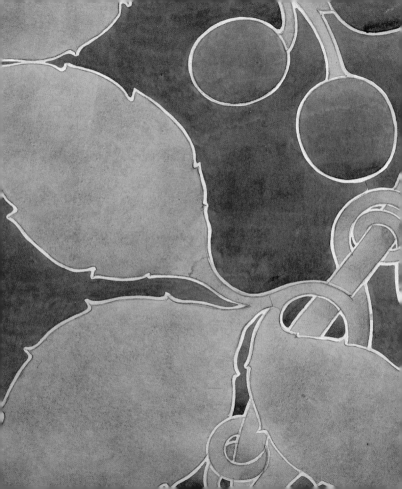

SEPTEMBER

MONDAY

8 FRIDAY

oliday, Canada (Labour Day) and USA (Labor Day)

TUESDAY

9 SATURDAY

WEDNESDAY

10 SUNDAY

THURSDAY

The 'Abbotsford No. 4' design for a printed textile by
C.F.A. Voysey (1857–1941). Pencil and watercolour on paper.
English, about 1897–1899.

ull Moon

SEPTEMBER

11 MONDAY

15 FRIDA

12 TUESDAY

16 SATURDA

13 WEDNESDAY

17 SUNDA

14 THURSDAY

Last Quarter

Earthenware tile with a relief design, manufactured
J.H. Barratt & Co., Stoke-on-Trent. English. 19(

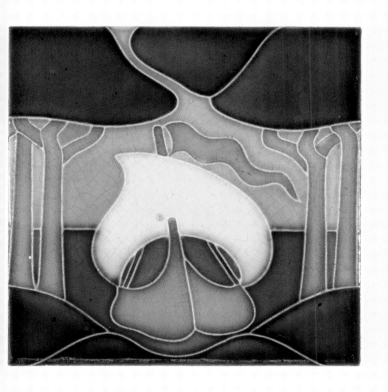

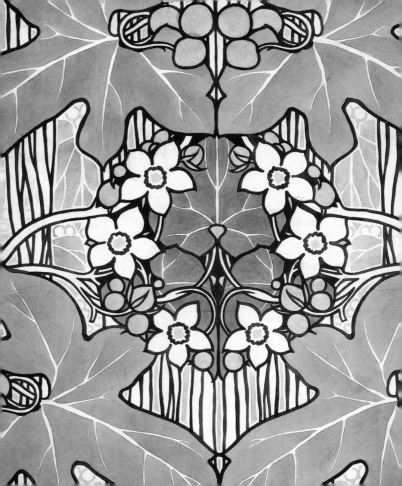

SEPTEMBER

8 MONDAY

22 FRIDAY

New Moon

9 TUESDAY

23 SATURDAY

Autumnal Equinox
Jewish New Year (Rosh Hashanah)

20 WEDNESDAY

24 SUNDAY

First Day of Ramadân (subject to sighting of the moon)

21 THURSDAY

The 'Bryony' design for a woven textile by Lindsay P. Butterfield
(1869–1948). Pencil and watercolour on paper. English, 1905.

SEPTEMBER/OCTOBER

25 MONDAY

29 FRIDA

Michaelmas Da

26 TUESDAY

30 SATURDA

First Quarte

27 WEDNESDAY

1 SUNDA

28 THURSDAY

Glassware, designed by Philip Webb (1831–1915) an
manufactured for Kelmscott Manor by James Powell & Son
London. English, about 186(

OCTOBER

MONDAY

6 FRIDAY

Jewish Day of Atonement (Yom Kippur)

TUESDAY

7 SATURDAY

Full Moon
Jewish Festival of Tabernacles (Succoth), First Day

WEDNESDAY

8 SUNDAY

THURSDAY

Design for a wallpaper or printed textile by
Lindsay P. Butterfield (1869–1948).
Pencil and watercolour on paper. English, 1903.

9 MONDAY

13 FRIDA

Holiday, Canada (Thanksgiving Day)
Holiday, USA (Columbus Day)

10 TUESDAY

14 SATURDA

Last Quarte
Jewish Festival of Tabernacles (Succoth), Eighth Da

11 WEDNESDAY

15 SUNDA

12 THURSDAY

Electroplated nickel-silver wine jug, designed b
Christopher Dresser (1834–1904) and produced b
Elkington & Co. English, 190

OCTOBER

16 MONDAY

20 FRIDAY

17 TUESDAY

21 SATURDAY

18 WEDNESDAY

22 SUNDAY

New Moon

19 THURSDAY

Design for printed velveteen by C.F.A. Voysey (1857–1941).
Watercolour on paper. English, 1888.

OCTOBER

23 MONDAY

27 FRIDAY

Holiday, New Zealand (Labour Day)

24 TUESDAY

28 SATURDAY

United Nations Day

25 WEDNESDAY

29 SUNDAY

First Quarter
British Summertime ends

26 THURSDAY

The 'Swan, Rush and Iris' design for a wallpaper
by Walter Crane (1845–1915). Body colour and
watercolour on paper. English, 1875.

OCTOBER/NOVEMBER

30 MONDAY

3 FRIDAY

Holiday, Republic of Ireland

31 TUESDAY

4 SATURDAY

Hallowe'en

WEDNESDAY

5 SUNDAY

Full Moon
Guy Fawkes' Day

All Saints' Day

THURSDAY

The 'Manxman' piano, designed by M.H. Baillie Scott
(1865–1945). Ebonized mahogany, carved wood, pewter,
mother-of-pearl and marquetry of stained woods, with
movement by John Broadwood & Sons Ltd and case
possibly also by Broadwood. English, designed in 1896,
made in 1902–1903.

NOVEMBER

6 MONDAY

10 FRIDA

7 TUESDAY

11 SATURDA

Holiday, Canada (Remembrance Da
and USA (Veterans' Da

8 WEDNESDAY

12 SUNDA

Last Quart
Remembrance Sunday, L

9 THURSDAY

Necklace, designed by Archibald Knox (1864–1933) as pa
of the 'Cymric' range for Liberty & Co. Gold set wi
mother-of-pearl and opals. English, about 190

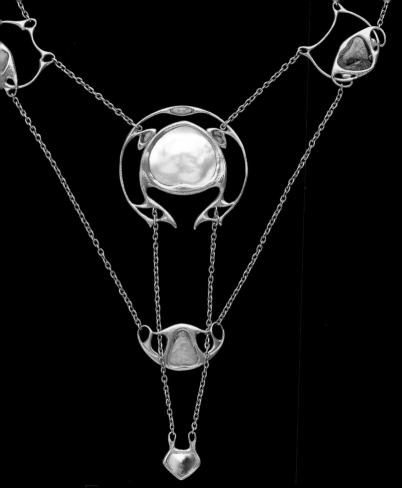

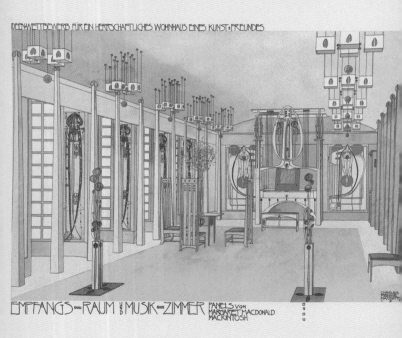

IDEEN-WETTBEWERB FÜR EIN HERRSCHAFTLICHES WOHNHAUS EINES KUNST-FREUNDES

EMPFANGS---RAUM UND MUSIK---ZIMMER PANELS VON MARGARET MACDONALD MACKINTOSH

NOVEMBER

3 MONDAY

17 FRIDAY

4 TUESDAY

18 SATURDAY

5 WEDNESDAY

19 SUNDAY

6 THURSDAY

Design for a music room by Charles Rennie Mackintosh
(1868–1928). 'House of an Art Lover', published by
Alex Koch, Darmstadt. Colour lithograph. German, 1901.

20 MONDAY

24 FRID,

New Moon

21 TUESDAY

25 SATURD,

22 WEDNESDAY

26 SUND,

23 THURSDAY

Furnishing textile, designed by Lewis Foreman D
(1845–1910) and made by Turnbull and Stockda
Roller-printed cotton. English, 188

Holiday, USA (Thanksgiving Day)

NOVEMBER/DECEMBER

27 MONDAY

1 FRIDAY

28 TUESDAY

2 SATURDAY

First Quarter

29 WEDNESDAY

3 SUNDAY

30 THURSDAY

Advent Sunday

Andrew's Day

Lead glazed earthenware vase made by the Wiener
Kunstkeramische Werkstätte, Vienna. Austrian, 1910.

DECEMBER

4 MONDAY

8 FRIDAY

5 TUESDAY

9 SATURDAY

Full Moon

6 WEDNESDAY

10 SUNDAY

7 THURSDAY

'The God of Love and Alceste. Chaucer's Goode Wimmer
Stained and painted glass panel, designed by Sir Edward Cole
Burne-Jones (1833–1898) and made for Morris, Marshall
Faulkner & Co. English, 1861–186

WEEK 50

DECEMBER

MONDAY

15 FRIDAY

2 TUESDAY

16 SATURDAY

1st Quarter

Jewish Festival of Chanukah, First Day

3 WEDNESDAY

17 SUNDAY

4 THURSDAY

Silver and gilt bowl, designed by Thorvald Bindesbøll
(1846–1908) and made by A. Michelsen. Danish, 1899.

18 MONDAY

22 FRID

Winter Solst

19 TUESDAY

23 SATURD

20 WEDNESDAY

24 SUND

New Moon

Christmas E

21 THURSDAY

The 'Favrile' vase, designed by Louis Comfort Tiffa
(1848–1933) and made by Tiffany Glass & Decorating C
Glass with metallic lustre. American, 1888–188

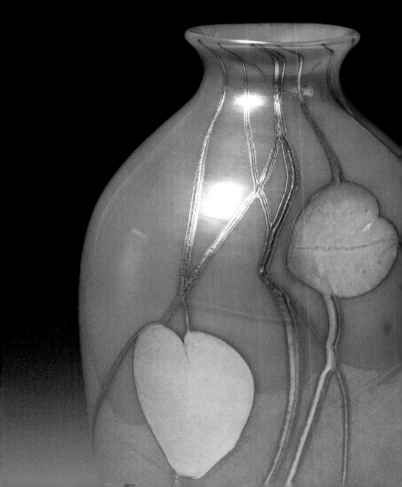

DECEMBER

5 MONDAY

Christmas Day
Holiday, UK, Republic of Ireland, Canada,
USA, Australia and New Zealand

5 TUESDAY

30 SATURDAY

Boxing Day (St Stephen's Day)
Holiday, UK, Republic of Ireland,
Canada, Australia and New Zealand

WEDNESDAY

31 SUNDAY

t Quarter

New Year's Eve

THURSDAY

Design for a wallpaper or printed textile by C.F.A. Voysey
(1857–1941). Pencil and watercolour on paper.
English, 1928.